A Million Ways To Measure The Sun

by

Steve Garside

Scanning, uploading and/or distribution of this book, or any designs or photographs contained therein, in whole or part (whether re-drawn, re-photographed or otherwise altered) via the Internet, CD, DVD, E-zine or photocopy without the express written permission of the copyright owner is illegal and punishable by law.

Poetry printed within this book © Steve Garside 2011.

Email stevegarside@hotmail.com
Website www.stevegarside.co.uk

Cover Art - © Nihad Wicho, 'Figures - Ink' 1990

Email - wichosryie@hotmail.fr

FOREWORD

'Steve Garside is a marvelously dexterous poet, whose poems provoke in me reactions that range from the heart-stopping to glee. His kaleidoscopic eye and his rigour with form are exemplary.'

Pete Kalu - Artistic Director, Commonword, Manchester.

'Steve's poetry is tightly observed and unwaveringly honest.'

Shamshad Khan - Poet

'Steve Garside - artist, poet and gritty visionary.'

John G. Hall - Poet, Editor, Spleen, Citizen 32.

Dedication

for my children, Elisabetta and Giorgia

CONTENTS

Title Track   7

I

The Paper Trees	10
The Chairs	11
No Beer	12
Rayaan	13
Epitaph	14
Non Sum Qualis Eram	15

II

The End	17
Forecast	18
Carbolic	20
Love Song Not Needed	21
Dead Letter Message	22
Domestic	23
Tin Foil Gerbil	24
Fallout Room	25
Helicopters	26
Our Teacher Took Photos Of Us	27
Portrait	28

III

Headlines	30
Experiments	31
The Oldest Trick	32
Psoriasis	34
Latitudes	35
Light	36
The Mills Are Dead	37
Dereliction	39
Nothing To Say	40
Invincible	41
the old Lie	42

IV

Verse 45	44
Here	45
Closer	46
Delicate	47
Exegesis	48
We	49
Per Ti Amore	50
You	51
For The Love of Love	52
Obsidian	53
Testament	54

V

Al Piede Della Montagna	56
Waiting for Water	57
Peaches	58
Cycles	59
Videotape	60
Five	61
Plot	62

list of publications   63

Title Track

Tell me more than the moon,
or give me more than the sun -

you say there's a million ways
to measure it - your eclipse

an upturned thumb -
blood-full from centuries

before vowels - mercurial plot
to the present pornography

of sound-byte. Consider again
the amulet gift of fingers -

elongated codes; cell-walled,
the undulating surface of identity;

exploring the continents of hands
in prayer, in childbirth, in flour,

or delving into someone else's pockets,
coaxing an escape from the duress

of small coins and stones,
crapshot for those unknown

shotgun scattergraph debtors,
discovered under shifting cloud covers.

Bring the mourners, the sitters;
those whose hands fold flags,

deliver soil, clutch lists -
lie through the skin of their sleep

from sunset to sunrise may they bleed,
while the moon, size constant; stays silent.

I

The Paper Trees

Flattering the sound of streams
in folds of breeze; the paper trees.

Equidistant lines of fifty in a field -
sunlight geo-divided by their honest bark.

No tree ever lied until brought down
and volume bound for another light.

And yet; cutlery is table set down
all over towns for the company of night.

So I smile, not needing to complete this rhyme
because the invisible is already perfect.

The Chairs

Twelve chairs in all;
none make the set.
Two neat rows
of obligatory etiquette.

Seats worn to
a relative shine,
suffocated fidgeting
as time beat time.

And what - if anything -
has ever been
resolved ever?

Her unreal hair.

The disorderly rosary.

Her marbled hands;
clasped as if of
alabaster - cold as
distant stars seem -
scattered indiscriminately,
like kisses, soil, or seed.

No Beer

There's no beer here Steve, no beer here.
No-one drink since he die.
Fridge empty, freezer full with ice.

My thoughts fidget for answers,
I move my feet a bit;
scratch grit against the concrete.

In the cellar; wine turn to vinegar
by the day, he says,

as I murmur Hail Mary for him,

and the moon - still up there,
but harvest not needed anymore.

Rayaan
(for Mahmood, his wife and family)

Before you died, I kissed your tiny forehead;
wished that life might pour from me
into you, so maybe you would one day
cradle me in the crook of your arm -
while I told you of the stave of kisses
you helped me to sing.

But we will never know
as the sky covers over with cloud
and the seas fill from unforgiving rivers.

For now, your cold lips are of myself,
the word, the breath, this prayer within.

Epitaph

Cold capitals are marble.
Column thick; ranks of names
Familiar as these fields; each with a plot

Preceding the next
And the next
And the next.

Whispers for more war
Persist the sabotage of ceasefire
Suggestions;

Leaves fall incessant
On lead white streets;
Furnish pavements and blow across roads

Or huddle on doorsteps;
Sun stunned at dawn like all these names;
Each citadel strong; weathering.

Non Sum Qualis Eram

I will not speak ill of the dead
nor weep of their sad undress in the face
of Life, or permit slight shadows cast that wreck
thoughts with venomous pause to shroud
fraudulent breath upon those already gone.

You will not either sell of the dead
or idle, needle-like inside their kaleidoscopic poise
blazed out upon the countenance of all majesty
announced from disparate rivers and divisions
blunt patricians would presume dictate.

We will not, with revolving appeal tarnish
their chiseled tenors with any unjust Wheel
nor sculpt unsettled earth with maleficence
and grim report of this Act through the eyes
of others as if tinkering on piano keys
in the house of some lamentable tune.

I will instead write as sailors rejoice their spoils
from some other innocent place, and with glad grace
regale your silent ways and journeys gathered,
the vast return of your sunsets given,
to breathe with ease of all incontrovertibly you,
for I am not now as once I was.

II

The End

Cold as this car park
Your fingertips tuned to war,
I hear the beat they share -
shudder at the silence of stone.

This old church has beaten me,
the grass stiff as your lips -
sweep me under the pews my love;
kiss me with a breath of soil,
then end me with your brow.

Forecast

Tomorrow

at 0600hrs,

all our children

should be considered.

Circular scars raised

1 cm diameter

lower left nipple

old corresponding

wound tissue

right anterior lower

rib cage -

several similar

upper left quadrant

right buttock.

Triangular mark

to central thorax

area fading -

latent swelling

lacerations

to lower spine

6cm's length

1cm width.

Linear 4cm marks
welted below
tibial tuberosity
on left leg
(bony prominence)
purple bruising
to second metacarpal
phalangeal joint
(the joint between
the hand and fingers)
old brown finger tip
bruising to upper
inner thighs -
parental response
inconsistent
no clear history given.

Carbolic

Words like these, operate with ease.
They probe and incise their competent knives
throughout the day within the night.

Clothes have grown slack as skin
while yearning to be touched -
though not touched.

In bed, my hip juts out;
the arc of a question mark

and I am lost.

The stench of disinfectant
never fails to connect

The stench of disinfectant
never fails to connect

The stench of disinfectant
never fails to connect;

though not cleanse.

Love Song Not Needed

Lie flat in a ditch and cover the body next to you
with polythene, curse the acoustics under the bridge
as you drag the corpse to a room of drawn curtains.

Wear a bald wall of distrust and poison the soil
with your spade of words, regard your neighbour
like a flanked spear; bull bloodied in your one eye.

Oust those roses while whistling white flags
from your twisted face; graze the ground; dig down
a fingertip at a time and bury that love song forever.

Dead Letter Message

Winter blistered white,
Frosted-grass-blades
Sear my naked skin
In this frozen soil.

Spade out my words,
As ice was as life is -
Table-set-crucifixions,
Fragments of tedium,
Incidental ambulances
Moaning through midnight.

Fold your napkin over my love;
perfect that pathetic lexicon of fate
while windows dawn, radios frustrate,
and satellites crackle in the depths of space.

Domestic

There was silence, excepting
this bliss of knife-blade-nerves;

water spinning, my face fishing
for reflection in the rain and snow.

Shaved potatoes, underwater swollen;
pale grenades in the washing-up bowl.

My bloodied nose; that bastard tree -
these fingers twisted with rosemary.

Your inflorescent oven heat ticks -
gloves me in; and then you grin,

leave the baby on the backstep my love
and let thy mothering commence.

Tin Foil Gerbil

We dug a hole for our tin foil gerbil,
placed pretend potato peel sentinels
at action stations in the soil;
ring fenced the burial with
a poisoned Salmon's entrails.

And waited.

We petrified toy soldiers
in guts of marmalade;
their plastic attitudes
amber'd behind scale sized tanks
from old wars;
where bayonets
punctured letters home in the chest;
stick pinning words to dead hearts.

We covered our face and hands
with someone else's clothing;
shut all windows fast -
scribbled a labelled name and wrapped
the corpse up tight and mourned,
mourned the radio coils warming to advise
when it would be safe to go outside.

Fallout Room

The safest spot was a white circle
within a tangerine coloured oblong:
sanctuary represented in shapes.

If anybody died in that space,
I had paper labels to hand
for name and address details
and a felt pen for permanence.

But when the attack was sounded
I was a full thirty years from home;
you on my shoulder; pleading,

my mother wanting a light
in the windy night;
family scattered across my face
like silver jacks, waiting

for the all clear to sound.

Helicopters
(for Mr Wright)

Each summer, the stink of books permit.
Dust specs perfect laconic universal ends.

Back then, the teacher, who would unpack
the night and ignite the wool
to save one coat from a cloakroom full,
checked his watch and retired.

goodbyes dissolved as sugar lumps do,
the books shelved absorbed the shock.

'The world will never be the same again,'
she said - pervading his desk...

écouter et répéter

This world will never be the same.

Our Teacher Took Photos Of Us

One taken on the towpath,
the other by the school gym;

both in black and white,
we was his first class after

Fisher, Dogger, German Bite
revision sessions were forgotten.

Cocksure kids; hair needing
a cut above the bridge - some

he stood on chairs to smile.
Before the dark end of teenage

slipped from bullying into heroin
and pissed through doorway bin bags,

our teacher took photos of us,
before his own child drowned.

Portrait

I pause to see your sketched parents
floating in charcoal.
Dad - bowler hatted,
Mum - hidden in her pinny:
both faceless at this distance.

Beneath them, your crayoned land and pram -
whispered with the same translucent lines
as the infant school and village hall;
four squat house blocks
with thin kinked chimney stack smoke,
where a crosshatched dog bares its teeth
in an agony of scratched lead; as death followed.

III

Headlines

They can rush any breakfast bar
Cupped in a fake tan sunrise.

Cloud fill epidural coffee shops
With clocks, logic and eyebrows,

And stand men in boy sized shadows.

Experiments

Can fizz shock circles
around a lab jug safe
for school children to see.

Scorching surface water;
science aimed on itself
can chemical surprise seconds
and traumatise for lifetimes.

The Oldest Trick

I sit; simmering.
My fingers shouldering
the nib across this page.

Left to right
left to right
left to right

keeping to the line.

If there is no break
I will cross magnificent
to the other side.

If the paper is truly
from a farmed tree
then it is pure -

nothing up its sleeve of bark
to blow a shiver of leaves over
my neighbour's path

I write a hundred times -
punctuating the page
for a reason spooled
in a news reel -

I am an animal
I am an animal
I am an animal

full stop.

Psoriasis

Was it him on Baltic Avenue, at the red hotel?
The door revolving, a murmured something
escaping from his beard. I couldn't be certain.

Crossing Vermont I realised like an itch which
strikes anywhere that Pennsylvania Station
was where, I swear, I saw him again -

(that eye of intent I could never forget,
having sneered at the tv so many times).

By the time I lost Indiana that infernal itch raged
like a campfire of needles - forcing my arms up my back
as if hostage to a crowd of invisible Indians -

so I glazed out across Pacific Structures and felt sure
I could hear some whisper grow within the rolling clouds
as shed locks were fist clutched like prisoners, and the night

delivered its verdict.

Latitudes

I am ink.

Nib-deep in this page;
quilting the vagaries of lines.

I beg for lead or felt tip pens
to carve myself out of alleyways;
cresting a crayon road to effervesce.

You must think it grows on trees, she says,
as the lines regroup to tightrope me in
while outside, the wind hop scotches continents.

Light

In this thousand dollar light
you look like you could nudge
your eye under the rim
of a crosswire sight.

In this thousand dollar light
your forehead lends
a mean grenade sheen -

borrows a brow of stormcloud
to syringe this mercury smile switch
for someone else in their million dollar day.

The Mills Are Dead

Backboned of redbrick,
guttural fuck from
the three day week,
the operation of bread
strike led darkness
scuffled end of the canal,
the mills are dead now mate;
the mills are dead.

These bones don't know
white finger, sluice-gated
pike faced, algae flushed
cheeks of the bar; after hours
poker hands, cribbage board
matchsticks; picking gristle
from Capstan teeth, kind of
open door neighbourhood kid,

Cos the mills are dead now mate,
the mills are dead.

But I reckon your mother would know -
sure as a fiver on the flags
of a Sunday morning, organ playing
Afro-Caribbean Lady - ginnel calling
her late husband to the pulse
of the cossack's daughter, shipped
over, shaving potatoes sobbing by the kitchen sink.

Cos the mills are dead now mate,
the mills are dead.

Dereliction

In this mist, the mills diminish.
Staved wire rusting; winter bemoaning
of its shivering length.

Helmets of frost crown concrete posts,
braced by the ice and stone of earth;
I imagine the rooftop siren's silence too;
resonating through these shadows of glass.

This frozen sluice won't release the ochre
from its veins, won't let me bleed wildly
onto this page, won't let me demolish you
like an industry, or leave you out
as a lost thought on a square white field.

All this redbrick weight-suffocates;
even in black and white it screams.
Don't cry, I hear you confess -
I could return to fold your Christmas napkins.

Hope is a word brimming with cement; sack lumped
from one lap to another; a handout doled out,
without music, without word, absolutely entropic -
dissolving in caustic circles below.

Nothing To Say

Once glimpsed; hate's guise encircles the soul.
This insidious sentinel strikes its camp
until mercenary thoughts like shadows come.

And what deeds are yet to be done
when man parades understanding
while the leopard senses the antelope?

So I have nothing to say about hatred,
as my words are but a distant murmur -
like a whispered request for more guns.

Invincible

I crouch; trench led to the bar by my blind friend,
my drink reflecting everyone lost to the night.

A dim window coloured corridor slopes away
to some other room of escaping laughter.

Ginnels are revealed with every filled glass of thought,
drug induced heart rushed youths fuck through their headlines

and wink a full stop finger of drink to invisible death.
I am no longer this my friend, I am no longer this.

the old Lie

Through your eyes I see myself. And if this day is to be the day then, I am the man you made of me, with love and pain inside of me, like concubines of sibling rivalry laid waste of this naked sketch, to drink from me and make me flesh again.

Through your eyes I see myself, as if to bleed my fruit to be, the vast mapped lands scattered discriminately, as once all were children; all again will remotely be.

Through your eyes I see myself; all ego, image and blunt intensity, to be torn to shreds like spent betting slips, while limp flags like shirt laps hang in silent yards.

Through your eyes I see now, and all my thoughts are as blank albums yet to be; spread out like a tablecloth for tea.

Yes, now your eyes hold our destiny, as I return home, to my wife, my children, and me.

IV

Verse 45

Your voice is amongst these trees,
quivering through cobwebs,
tickling leaves with your breath,
giving life to a fire of silences.

Here

Chiffon floats like the surface of the sea in me,
and through this open window waits
lost words dispersed as you are not here with me.

Not with the Earth and all of its ends
not with the sentiment of some silent
carving pressed onto fate;
like death ultimately is.

The caress of your breath
the sanctuary of your breast
the distance of the unclaimed day.

Closer

You kissed me today on the cheek of our yesterdays.
Your words arriving warm like a taxi flagged on a winter's night.

Of all our goodbyes, I miss you most in this moment;
my fingertips lost without the trace of your skin.

The infused essence of you dissipates my senses,
like a sated crowd dispersing, and I'm left here -
rehearsing, rehearsing, rehearsing.

Delicate

We sat with the sun on our backs.
I'd not changed a bit; you said you liked that.

Khaki somehow, I've never grown out of -
though I no longer run with bricks in a rucksack.

Young men on mountain bikes pass; a dog walker dips
with a bag. The lake, absorbing the morning, cradles the sky.

I linger most days in thought of you I say;
I linger most days in thought.

Exegesis

What left of love is yet unsaid
within this breath of you?
Tonight we lie like question marks
as lovers sometimes do.

In separate rooms we ask the quiet;
you of him, me of her, they of them -
is all we ever wished to hold
to play ourselves without?

Outside this quilted world of wait
the dawn's neat edge draws near
can one sweet sacrifice of youth
forgive these coming years?

And here this frost clutched frame
of us denies all guest but fate,
I sit and learn as lovers do
with words to fit this room.

I sit and learn as lovers do
with words to fit this room.

We

Are similar thinkers; sofa sunk
in a bar our fingers tingle.

Glass bottomed missed smiles
borrowed from other lover's faces

shape your eye.

You're closer now than before; a little closer;
as a lush pulse of blood shovels my heart

to my hands.

Per Ti, Amore

I sketched a star
and vaulted space;
sang a moon into orbit
to cool my tides;
so restless this breathing
in the thought of your being.

From this wish of art
I can only weep -
offering you my sad hands opened,
to cradle my words, naked on this page.

You

Edge the tide of your sex
veil-warmed over my breath.

Coastal-thrusting into nothing;
you cast your diamonds and gold

helmed from the corpse of oceanic others
you swell, pupil-like in horizon light,

while their chorus whispers snuggle
the sail of this virtual night; trusting.

For The Love Of Love

For the love of love I hold no measure.
I scrawl by lamplit midnight in this room
Where no hearthplace beckons
Or cinnamon crackles through the grate.

No shadows glance up these blank page walls
To suggest a life that you could grace -
My failing faith reserves for you a space
Dull mooned in any tea cup stained
Or history lent to picture frames
Of just caught smiles and half won days.

For the breath of you of the breath of me
Entwined like a birthday bow of hushed eaves,
Fills my idle waking hours of wait
Until this happy smile of youth aches of waste.

Will you ever know the windows of my refrain
Whilst fast within moments held close
As silence dressed of years' ends unseen;
Untouched like books boxed
For the pound shop of passed on dreams;
Their chapters relenting together
As the sun drains into clouds outside
And the darklights pool my hushing breath home
For this burning night to begin.

Obsidian

In these hands I held a stone.
Each cool face coveted;
it lent nothing only shadow,
like a child cornering the sea.

Sunlight will free it, I thought -
opening my eyes at dawn,

though without a ripple
it sank, insignificant as silt
with the pulse of a dead star.

Testament

Yours is the longest night;
remote as the sky from my fingers.

I feel you move throughout each day unheld,
simple words build my paper wishes.

I am your neck, your exquisite thighs,
a simple star kissed on your silent face.

V

Al Piede Della Montagna

Once yearly; early morning,
we walk in the mountains of his youth.

We get there by car; an hour's silent drive
up winding roads shadowed toward sunrise.

When we arrive, he tells me again about the brickworks
of card games won once and wedding envelopes -

times I never breathed though now know so well.

Goats bells distance themselves in the surrounding hills
as we root for porchini and the ever elusive truffle.

Later we'll sit under a tree as the sun strengthens its arc;
eat sandwiches, drink his wine, make a small fire -

and laugh about the tale that only he survives to tell.

Waiting For Water

When you arrive
there is always time
for conversation.

The taps are on
from 8 'til 10.

People get here
early - sit on crates;
share platitudes -
waterpipes readied
to smooth the flow
from one bottle
to another.

Once, there was a fella,
he retired now,
was a fuckin' bastard him,
he put tap on at 8 -
but slow, like piss.

Others nod, unscrewing bottle tops -
but then the water rush arrives
and everyone hubbubs; shifting caskets;
while their chatter ascends into song.

Peaches

He picked them from a nearby field unseen -
mid-afternoon while church tower shadows grew.

Empty bag stuffed into his pocket, with a wink
he was gone into the sun; hiding under hazelnut trees.

As the dogs dozed by the outside sink, and the cats'
patience measured seconds with their snaking tails

he returned; with a bagful. Leaning over to tip their weight,
the peaches tumbled out, filling the washing up bowl.

Their skins cooling in the shade of the lemon tree,
we sifted through the ripe fruit, tossing one or two aside,

then gathered the rest; spread the dining room table inside -
those peaches compliment his red wine like moments do in time.

Every year they brim-fill our car, as the hour becomes the hour,
in August, all roads home are hot and the peaches always turn sour.

Cycles

After my father died, I was fifteen.
I went to work in cycle shop, he says
as I hand him a spanner.

His garage is full of bottled sauce,
wine and plum tomatoes; trays of beans
cusping in the window by the door.

I fix bikes all time for food to eat -
my mother was a very busy woman.

You know how many bikes I got in attic?
Six - all bigger sizes than this one, he says
removing the stabilisers; placing them
in a fruit crate filled with dusty bolts,
hazelnuts and disused cobwebs.

Children growing up everyday Steve -
everyday children growing up.

Videotape

There's a photograph of this moment
I put it on a t-shirt - a gift to my father from me.

There's this videotape too -
he's cradling our baby in the crook of his arm,
where a bucket is slung, for the beans he picks.

The long fat pods budge in the bucket bottom,
plucked from the spindly vine,

She try to put beans in her mouth she does,
she try to put beans in her mouth.

He sings this phrase over and over
as I stop, rewind and play,
stop, rewind and play.

Five

The last hours of being five
Arrive, as I carry you to bed.

You ask: is that me in your arms
As a baby daddy? Yes it is Love,
Not looking over my shoulder
At the photo to face the past,

Yes it is - I could hold you
In my forearm then, I say,
And now you fill my breath
At the top of the stairs.

I tuck you in.
Tomorrow,
You will be six, I say.

We smile as you snuggle
Your bear, all tucked in,
And close your eyes,
To the last hours
Of being five.

Plot

And the stones spoke of death
as the grass shivered its mane
to the sea and morning sun;
while the trees just swayed
without saying a word.

List of Publications

The Paper Trees	-	The Tower Journal, Winter 2010-11,
Peaches		Vol. 3 Num.2
The Oldest Trick		www.thetowerjournal.com
Light		
Delicate		

The Chairs	-	The Strand Book of International Poets,
Exegesis		2010, Strand UK, London,
		ISBN 9781907340062

The Mills Are Dead	-	The Spleen, Ed - John G. Hall, 2010,
Tin Foil Gerbil		Militant Minds, UK,
the old Lie		ISBN 978-1-4467-1752-3
Helicopters		

Here	-	Whispers on the Breeze Anthology, 2009, United Press, UK, ISBN 978-1-84436-905-8
Forecast	-	Other Poetry, Series 4, Issue 2, 2010, Tyneside Free Press, UK, ISBN 0144 5847
Fallout Room	-	Other Poetry, Series 4, Issue 3, 2011 Tyneside Free Press, UK, ISBN

www.ingramcontent.com/pod-product-compliance
Lightning Source LLC
Chambersburg PA
CBHW061250040426
42444CB00010B/2329